Draw & Solve Word Problems

Rob Madell and Laura Zoe Dombrowski

Modeling Word Problems for **Addition and Subtraction within 20**

Printed in the United States of America.

This book is printed on recycled paper.

Order Number 211270
ISBN 978-1-58324-729-7

A B C D E 22 21 20 19 18

395 Main Street
Rowley, MA 01969
www.didax.com

Contents

Introduction

The ability to model word problems is the basis of all of whole-number arithmetic. The Math Standards define 11 different types of word problems that children are expected to be able to model by the end of Grade 1. Here is an example of one of those types.

Put Together/Total Unknown

> 9 apples are in a tree.
>
> 7 apples are on the grass.
>
> How many apples are there in all?

We might teach children to model this problem with counters:

1. Show me the 9 counters that will be the apples in the tree.
2. Show me the 7 counters that will be the apples on the grass.
3. Put the apples together and count how many there are altogether.

We might also teach children to model this problem with paper and pencil:

1. Draw 9 small circles that will be the apples in the tree.
2. Draw 7 small circles that will be the apples on the grass.
3. Count how many apples there are altogether.

This book, together with the others in the series, is intended to help children model the Math Standards problem types with paper and pencil. The 11 types that are required by the end of Grade 1 are included here in this volume.

How to Use This Book

Start by reminding yourself of the 11 different problem types that children are expected to learn to model by the end of Grade 1.

The Introduction to Addition discusses the four types of addition problems, and the Introduction to Subtraction discusses the seven types of subtraction problems.

Next, introduce your students to solving new types of word problems with physical models. Use counters or other manipulatives for demonstrations and discussions with the whole group, with small groups, and ideally with individual children.

At some later point you can introduce paper-and-pencil models and then have children work largely on their own with the worksheets provided here. Paper-and-pencil models have at least one advantage over physical models. At the end of class you will be able to collect and review each student's work.

Take From/Change Unknown - 3

Name

There are 9 seeds.
A bird eats some.
There are 6 seeds left.
How many seeds did the bird eat? 3

1 2 3 4 5 6 7 8 9

© Didax, Inc. Draw & Solve Word Problems 57

First-grade students easily learn to make simple drawings. Circles can represent chickens. The letter *P* can represent a pig. Here seeds are represented very simply—by small dots.

We have used worksheets like these with our students and are happy with the results. We hope that you have a similar experience.

A Note About Names

In writing here about the various problem types, we have used the names assigned to those types by the Math Standards. But the only names that we use with our students are *addition*, *subtraction*, *multiplication*, and *division*. We do sometimes make the distinction, for example, between "one type of addition problem" and "another type of addition problem."

A Note About Modeling

Eventually children will learn to represent word problems with equations, and to solve those word problems, and to solve those equations, with strategies beyond counting. For example, the problem about apples can be represented by the equation

$$9 + 7 = \square$$

and can be solved by reasoning that since 7 + 7 = 14, then 9 + 7 must equal 16. But first children must learn what these word problems mean—in this case that the apples should be put together and counted one by one. These books are about teaching children what word problems mean.

A Note About Drawing

Some children like to make elaborate drawings. For the problem about apples, they may want to draw apples with stems, trees with leaves, and flowers growing in the grass. They may even want to draw the sun and clouds. But none of this detail is essential to the mathematics. In fact, the Standards of Mathematical Practice encourage teachers to help children to "*decontextualize*—to abstract a given situation and represent it symbolically . . ." These books support that standard. We think that you should encourage children to make very simple drawings.

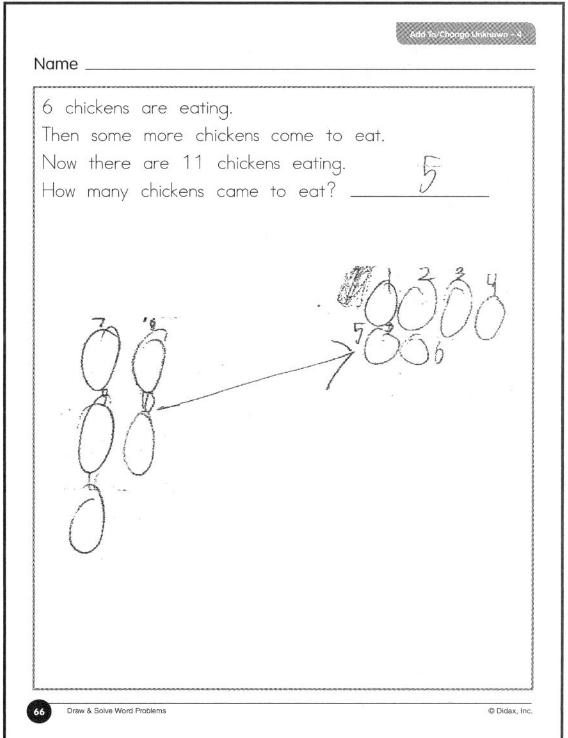

Add To/Change Unknown – 4

Name

6 chickens are eating.
Then some more chickens come to eat.
Now there are 11 chickens eating.
How many chickens came to eat? 5

66 Draw & Solve Word Problems © Didax, Inc.

An advantage of drawings over manipulatives is that they leave a record of how the child solved the problem. It is clear that this child counted out 6 "chickens," then counted out more until he got to 11, then counted out how many he had added to the original 6.

A Note About Understanding vs. Memorizing

Some children come to school understanding some types of word problems. **Add To/Result Unknown** is a good example. Other types of word problems can be difficult for children. T**ake From/ Start Unknown** and **Compare/Bigger Unknown** are good examples. To help them we advocate direct instruction in modeling. But to be clear, we are not arguing for mechanical, rote learning. We merely believe in putting difficult problems in front of children and helping them to understand those problems. We don't advocate having them memorize steps that they do not understand.

A Note About Reading

We have tried to make the word problems in this book as easy to read as possible. We hope that this allows for the challenge of the word problems to be mathematical rather than one of reading. A complete list of all the words used can be found in the word list on page 95.

But in your class discussion we suggest that you restate the problems to sound more natural. For example, where a problem reads,

> 2 ducks sit in the grass.
>
> 3 more ducks come to sit in the grass.
>
> How many ducks are in the grass now?

you might say instead,

> 2 ducks were sitting in the grass.
>
> Then 3 more ducks came to sit with them.
>
> How many ducks are in the grass now?

—Rob Madell and Laura Dombrowski

Introduction to Addition

The Math Standards define 11 different types of word problems that children are expected to be able to model by the end of Grade 1. Of these 11, four involve addition.

Children need to be helped to see that in spite of important differences among these four types, each can be understood as the joining of two sets of objects, and each can be solved by counting the objects in the joined sets altogether. That is why the same strategies and algorithms can be used to solve all four types of problems.

Add To/Result Unknown

A boy had 4 dolls.

Then his sister gave him 7 more dolls.

How many dolls does the boy have now?

Put Together/Total Unknown

4 pigs are in the mud.

7 pigs are on the grass.

How many pigs are there altogether?

These two types of word problems are typically introduced in Kindergarten—usually with sums less than 10. Most children have little difficulty learning to model them. The steps in making those models are identical.

Step	Add To/ Result Unknown	Put Together/ Total Unknown
1	Draw the 4 dolls the boy had.	Draw the 4 pigs in the mud.
2	Draw the 7 dolls his sister gave to him.	Draw the 7 pigs on the grass.
3	Count the dolls altogether.	Count the pigs altogether.

In the pages that follow, you will find examples with sums as large as 20. **Add To/Result Unknown** problems begin on page 3 and are followed by **Put Together/Total Unknown** problems, beginning on page 11.

Take From/Start Unknown

Some cats were sitting on a bed.

4 of the cats jumped off the bed onto the floor.

Then 7 cats were still on the bed.

How many cats were on the bed at first?

Help your students to visualize a "mental movie" of the scene that this problem describes. At the end of that movie there are 7 cats sitting on a bed and there are an additional 4 cats on the floor. Then help them to roll that movie backwards. At the start of the movie the 4 cats on the floor are on the bed. Before those 4 jumped off the bed, there were $7 + 4 = 11$ cats on the bed.

So this really is an addition problem! A hard addition problem! It is hard because it is hard to play that movie backwards. It is even hard to understand that you *should* play the movie backwards.

We can help children to imagine the movie by helping them to model the problem following these steps:

1. Draw the 7 cats that are still on the bed.
2. Draw the 4 cats that jumped off the bed.
3. Count the cats that were on the bed at first.

Take From/Start Unknown problems begin on page 27.

Teaching Tip

Play the Movie Forward – Some children will try to solve this problem by playing the movie forward. You may even want to encourage that. At the start of the movie there are some cats on the bed—but we don't know how many. Some children may say, "What take away 4 equals 7?" Other children may even write the equation $\square - 4 = 7$. To help these children solve the problem, have them guess at what that missing number is—and have them check to see if they are right. Doing that is a good introduction to algebra and may help children to play the movie backward. But, playing it backward is what is important if children are to see the problem as an example of addition. Only when the movie is played backward will they see that the two sets of cats can be joined together and counted to solve the problem.

Compare/Bigger Unknown

A little dog ate 4 dog treats.

A big dog ate 7 more treats than the little dog.

How many treats did the big dog eat?

This type of problem also turns out to be difficult for children to understand. Many of them interpret "a big dog ate 7 more treats than the little dog" to mean that the big dog ate *exactly* 7 treats. Somehow they don't understand what those words really mean.

There is a big difference between modeling Compare/Bigger Unknown problems and modeling all the other addition problems. Whether acted out with physical objects or represented with paper and pencil, there must be 15 dog treats in any proper representation of this problem—not 11, as in the models above. (But it is still an addition problem because the treats that the big dog ate are the 4 that match what the little dog ate, together with 7 more.)

Here are the steps of this model.

1. Draw 4 treats for the little dog.
2. Draw 4 treats for the big dog so that she has the same number of treats as the little dog.
3. Draw 7 more treats for the big dog.
4. Count how many treats the big dog has.

Compare/Bigger Unknown problems begin on page 27.

Take From/Start Unknown - 3

Name

Some cows are in the barn.
3 of them go out.
There are 7 cows left in the barn.
How many cows were in the barn at first? 10

© Didax, Inc. Draw & Solve Word Problems 21

A very simple representation of 7 cows in a barn and 3 cows outside the barn—the scene at the end of the "movie." All the essential information has been captured.

Compare/Bigger Unknown - 1

Name

6 pigs are on a farm.
There are 2 more cows than pigs.
How many cows are on the farm? 8

© Didax, Inc. Draw & Solve Word Problems 27

This is a good example of the results of direct instruction in modeling. We taught the children to use P's and C's to represent pigs and cows. And we taught them to start by showing the same number of pigs as cows.

Name ______________________________

6 birds sit in a tree.

3 more birds fly there.

How many birds are in the tree now? ____________

Name ____________________

A man has 4 eggs.
He gets 6 more eggs.
How many eggs does he have now? ________

Name ____________________

5 rabbits sit in the grass.

3 more rabbits hop to them.

How many rabbits are in the grass now? __________

Name ______________________________

A horse ate 3 apples.
Then she ate 4 more apples.
How many apples did she eat in all? ______________

Name ___________________________

1. 9 girls are in the garden.

   8 more girls come to the garden.

   How many girls are in the garden now? ________

2. A boy has 8 toy boats.

   His mother gives him 8 more boats.

   How many boats does the boy have now? ________

Name ______________________________

1. 3 children are playing in the snow.
   9 more children come to play.
   How many children are playing now? ____________

2. 11 pigs are eating.
   7 more pigs come to eat.
   How many pigs are eating now? ____________

Name ______________________________

1. 12 cats ran up a tree.
   Then 3 more cats ran up the tree.
   How many cats are in the tree now? __________

2. A boy has 13 toys.
   He gets 6 more toys.
   How many toys does he have now? __________

Name ______________________________

1. A farmer has 10 cows.
   He gets 3 more cows.
   How many cows does the farmer have now? ______

2. A girl has 9 dolls.
   She finds 5 more dolls.
   How many dolls does she have now? ______

Name ____

3 bears eat.

6 bears sleep.

How many bears are there in all? ______________

Name ______________________________

5 birds are in a tree.

5 cats are in the tree.

How many animals are in the tree in all? __________

Name ______________________________

6 boys run.

2 girls jump.

How many children are there in all? ____________

Name ______________________________

2 black cars are in the street.

5 white cars are in the street.

How many cars are in the street? ____________

Name ____________________

1. 9 apples are in a tree.
   7 apples are on the grass.
   How many apples are there in all? __________

2. A black chicken has 4 eggs.
   A brown chicken has 8 eggs.
   How many eggs do they have in all? __________

Name ______________________________

1. 11 red flowers are in a garden.
   4 yellow flowers are in the garden.
   How many flowers are there in all? __________

2. 9 squirrels are on a hill.
   10 squirrels are in a tree.
   How many squirrels are there in all? __________

Name ______________________________

1. A girl makes 12 big cakes and 5 little cakes.
   How many cakes does she make in all? __________

2. A black bird ate 9 seeds.
   A blue bird ate 9 seeds.
   How many seeds did they eat in all? __________

Name ______________________________

1. 3 big ducks are in the water.
   11 baby ducks are in the water.
   How many ducks are in the water? __________

2. A big dog sees 8 red balls.
   A little dog sees 5 blue balls.
   How many balls did they see in all? __________

Name ______________________________

Some toys are on the floor.

A boy puts 4 of them on a table.

There are 2 toys left on the floor.

How many toys were on the floor at first? __________

Name ______________________________

Some chairs are at school.
A girl takes 5 of them home.
There are 3 chairs left at school.
How many chairs were at school at first? ___________

Name ______________________________

Some cows are in the barn.

3 of them go out.

There are 7 cows left in the barn.

How many cows were in the barn at first? __________

Name ______________________________

Some squirrels are in a tree.
2 of them run away.
There are 7 squirrels left in the tree.
How many squirrels were in the tree at first? ________

Name ______________________________

1. Some cats are in the house.
   5 of the cats go out.
   There are 8 cats left in the house.
   How many cats were in the house at first? ______

2. Some dolls are on a table.
   A boy takes 11 of them away.
   There are 5 dolls left on the table.
   How many dolls were on the table at first? ______

Name ______________________________

1. A man had some seeds.
   A bird ate 10 of them.
   There were 7 seeds left.
   How many seeds did the man have at first? ______

2. Some rings are on a chair.
   A man puts 9 of them on the table.
   There are 5 rings left on the chair.
   How many rings were on the chair at first? ______

Name ____________________

1. Some toy boats are in a box.
   A baby takes 12 of them out of the box.
   There are 7 boats left in the box.
   How many boats were in the box at first? ________

2. Some horses are playing in the rain.
   13 of them go into the barn.
   There are 5 horses left playing.
   How many horses were playing at first? ________

Name ______________________________

1. Some boys are eating at the table.
   6 of them go out to play.
   There are 6 boys left at the table.
   How many boys were at the table at first? ______

2. Some dogs are on a boat.
   3 of them jump into the water.
   There are 12 dogs left on the boat.
   How many dogs were on the boat at first? ______

Name ______________________________

4 pigs are on a farm.

There are 4 more cows than pigs.

How many cows are on the farm? ____________

Name ______________________________

There are 5 red balls.

There are 4 more yellow balls than red balls.

How many yellow balls are there? ____________

Name ______________________________

There are 3 little cakes.

There are 2 fewer little cakes than big cakes.

How many big cakes are there? ______________

Name ______________________________

There are 4 cats in the house.
There are 3 fewer cats than dogs.
How many dogs are in the house? ______________

Name ______________________________

1. There are 7 squirrels.

   There are 5 more birds than squirrels.

   How many birds are there? ____________

2. There are 5 brown horses.

   There are 3 more black horses than brown horses.

   How many black horses are there? ____________

Name ______________________________

1. There are 4 tables.

   There are 7 more chairs than tables.

   How many chairs are there? ____________

2. 7 boys sit on the floor.

   There are 6 more girls than boys on the floor.

   How many girls are on the floor? ____________

Name ______________________________

1. There are 7 red fish.

   There are 2 fewer red fish than blue fish.

   How many blue fish are there? ______________

2. There are 6 girls.

   There are 4 fewer girls than boys.

   How many boys are there? ______________

Name ______________________________

1. There are 2 chickens on a farm.
   There are 5 fewer chickens than sheep.
   How many sheep are on the farm? ____________

2. There are 7 ducks in the water.
   There are 7 fewer ducks in the water than on the grass.
   How many ducks are on the grass? ____________

Introduction to Subtraction

The Math Standards define 11 different types of word problems that children are expected to be able to model by the end of Grade 1. Of those 11, seven involve subtraction.

Children need to be helped to see that in spite of important differences among these seven, each can be understood as removing some of the objects from a set, and each can be solved by counting the objects that remain. That is why the same strategies and algorithms can be used to solve all seven types of problems.

Take From/Result Unknown

13 apples were on the table.

I ate 5 of the apples.

How many apples are on the table now?

Take Apart/Addend Unknown

13 apples are on the table.

5 of the apples are red and the rest are green.

How many apples are green?

These two types of word problems are typically introduced in Kindergarten—usually with numbers less than 10. Most children have little difficulty learning to model them. The steps in making those models are identical.

Step	Take From/ Result Unknown	Take Apart/ Addend Unknown
1	Draw the 13 apples.	Draw the 13 apples.
2	Show which 5 apples were eaten.	Show the 5 apples that are red.
3	Count the apples that are left.	Count the apples that are green.

Take From/Result Unknown problems happen over time and explicitly describe the separating of a set into two parts. **At the start**, 13 apples were on the table. **Then** I ate 5 of the apples.

Take Apart/Addend Unknown problems describe a set **(the 13 apples)** that has two parts **(the red apples** and **the green apples).** Nothing happens over time, and nothing is said about these two parts physically separating from one another.

In spite of these distinctions, the chart above shows that there is little or no difference in the way these problems are modeled.

In the pages that follow you will find examples with numbers as large as 20. **Take From/Result Unknown** problems begin on page 39 and are followed by **Take Apart/AddendUnknown** problems, beginning on page 47.

Take From/Change Unknown

13 apples were on the table.

I ate some of the apples.

Then there were 5 apples left.

How many apples did I eat?

As with the problems above, most children will have little trouble with the first step in making the model. They should draw the 13 apples. But some children may need help in understanding that the set of 13 apples consists of some that were eaten and some that are still left on the table. To find out how many were eaten, they should first remove the ones that are left.

Here are the steps of this model.

1. Draw the 13 apples.
2. Show which 5 apples are left.
3. Count the apples that were eaten.

Take From/Change Unknown problems begin on page 55.

Teaching Tip 1

Introduction to Algebra – After drawing the 13 apples, some children will want to guess at how many apples were eaten. They may even write the equation 13 – □ = 5. That is a good introduction to algebra and should be encouraged. But it is more important for first-graders that they see this problem as an example of a subtraction problem—and that requires them to see that to find the apples that were eaten they can take away the apples that are left.

Add To/Change Unknown

5 brown squirrels were in a tree.

Then some black squirrels ran up the tree.

Now there are 13 squirrels in the tree.

How many black squirrels ran up the tree?

Add To/Start Unknown

Some brown squirrels were in a tree.

Then 5 black squirrels ran up the tree.

Now there are 13 squirrels in the tree.

How many brown squirrels are in the tree?

Help your students to imagine two short movies picturing the events in these two problems. Both movies start with some brown squirrels in a tree. Then, in both movies, some black squirrels run up the tree. Both movies end with 13 squirrels in the tree—some black, and some brown. The way to model each of these problems is to start with the scene at the end of the movie.

Step	Add To/Change Unknown	Add To/Start Unknown
1	Draw the 13 squirrels in the tree.	Draw the 13 squirrels in the tree.
2	Show the 5 squirrels that are brown.	Show the 5 squirrels that are black.
3	Count the squirrels that are black.	Count the squirrels that are brown.

So in spite of the names of these two problem types, they are both subtraction problems—to solve them, some of the squirrels have to be taken away from the set of all 13 squirrels.

Add To/Change Unknown problems begin on page 63 and are followed by **Add To/Start Unknown** problems, beginning on page 71.

Teaching Tip 2

More Algebra – The two problems about squirrels can be represented by the equations 5 + □ = 13 and □ + 5 = 13, respectively. Some children may want to think about problems like these in that way. As above, thinking in this way is a good introduction to algebra, and we believe that it should be encouraged. On the other hand, as first-graders, it is more important that they see why both problems can be solved by subtraction. Subtraction works because both involve "taking away."

Compare/Difference Unknown

There are 13 brown squirrels.

There are 5 black squirrels.

How many more brown squirrels are there than black squirrels?

Help children to model this problem by following these steps. Their drawing should show 18 squirrels.

1. Draw the 13 brown squirrels.
2. Draw the 5 black squirrels.
3. Show which of the brown squirrels match the 5 black squirrels.
4. Count the extra brown squirrels.

Compare/Difference Unknown problems begin on page 79.

Compare/Smaller Unknown

There are 13 brown squirrels.

There are 5 more brown squirrels than black squirrels.

How many black squirrels are there?

To understand that this is a subtraction problem, children need to see that some of those 13 brown squirrels correspond to the black squirrels and that the rest of those brown squirrels are "extra." To find the number of black squirrels, they need to "take away" those 5 extras. You can help them by teaching them to model the problem with these steps.

1. Draw the 13 brown squirrels.
2. Show which of those brown squirrels are the 5 extra ones.
3. Count the remaining brown squirrels. (There are 8.)
4. Draw the 8 black squirrels.

Teaching Tip 3

Why Is This Subtraction? Steps 2 and 3 are very important. When children show which of the brown squirrels are "extra," and when they count the remaining brown squirrels, they are helped to think about why this is a subtraction problem. Their pictures should help them to see that we are "taking away" 5 from 13.

Compare/Smaller Unknown problems begin on page 87.

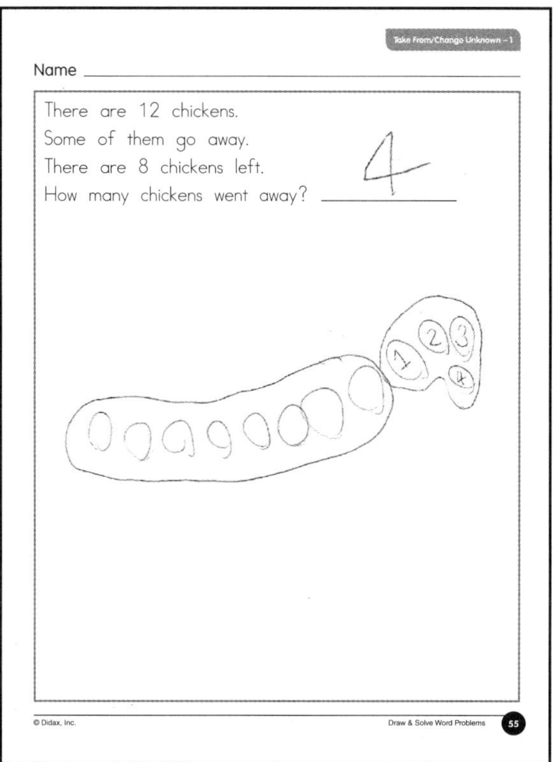

This child started with a very simple representation of the 12 chickens. To find how many went away, she circled the 8 chickens that did not go away.

Name ______________________________

There are 10 chickens.
5 of them go away.
How many chickens are there now? ____________

Name ______________________________

8 sheep are eating grass.

6 of them stop eating.

How many sheep are eating now? ____________

Name ______________________________

7 cats are in the house.

4 of them go out.

How many cats are in the house now? ____________

Name ____________________

A boy has 9 flowers.
He gives 3 of them to his father.
How many flowers does the boy have now? ________

Name ____________________

1. There are 15 chairs at school.
   The children take 8 of them home.
   How many chairs are at school now? ________

2. 17 squirrels are in a tree.
   11 of them jump to the ground.
   How many squirrels are in the tree now? ________

Name ____________________

1. 13 rings are in a box.
   A man takes 6 of them out of the box.
   How many rings are in the box now? __________

2. 12 toys are in the house.
   A girl puts 4 of them in the garden.
   How many toys are in the house now? __________

Name ____

1. 18 cows are in the barn.
   12 of them go for a walk.
   How many cows are in the barn now? ___________

2. 11 children play in the woods.
   They see a bear and 5 of them run home.
   How many children are in the woods now? ___________

Name ____________________

1. There are 19 robins.

   When they see a man, 7 of them fly away.

   How many robins are there now? __________

2. There are 14 rabbits.

   5 of them hop away.

   How many rabbits are there now? __________

Name ______________________________

There are 8 boys.

5 of them are eating.

The rest are sleeping.

How many boys are sleeping? ____________

Name ______________________________

There are 10 bears.

6 of them are brown.

The rest are black.

How many bears are black? ______________

Name ______________________________

There are 9 eggs.
5 of them are brown.
The rest are white.
How many eggs are white? ____________

Name ______________________________

There are 8 pets.
6 of them are dogs.
The rest are cats.
How many cats are there? ____________

Name ______________________________

1. There are 18 flowers.
   8 of them are red.
   The rest are yellow.
   How many flowers are yellow? ______________

2. There are 16 rabbits.
   9 of them hop.
   The rest walk.
   How many rabbits walk? ______________

Name ______________________________

1. There are 14 animals.
   8 of them are cows.
   The rest are pigs.
   How many pigs are there? ____________

2. There are 19 fish.
   14 of them are big.
   The rest are little.
   How many little fish are there? ____________

Name ____________________

1. There are 17 cars.
   8 of them are red.
   The rest are blue.
   How many cars are blue? ____________

2. There are 13 toy boats.
   7 of the boats are big.
   The rest are little.
   How many little boats are there? ____________

Name ______________________________

1. There are 15 cows.
   9 of them are brown.
   The rest are white.
   How many cows are white? ______________

2. There are 12 chickens.
   5 of them run.
   The rest walk.
   How many chickens walk? ______________

Name ______________________________

There are 6 apples.

A girl eats some of them.

There are 3 apples left.

How many apples did the girl eat? ____________

Name ______________________________

5 dogs are playing.

Some run away.

1 dog is left playing.

How many dogs ran away? ______________

Name ______________________________

There are 9 seeds.

A bird eats some.

There are 6 seeds left.

How many seeds did the bird eat? ______________

Name ________________________________

7 squirrels are in the garden.
Some go up a tree.
2 squirrels are left in the garden.
How many squirrels are in the tree? ______________

Name ______________________________

1. 17 toys are on the table.
   A boy takes some away.
   5 toys are left on the table.
   How many toys did the boy take? ____________

2. There are 11 rings in a box.
   A girl puts some of them on the table.
   8 rings are left in the box.
   How many rings are on the table? ____________

Name ______________________________

1. 16 girls are jumping.
   Some of them stop and sit.
   7 girls are left jumping.
   How many girls stopped? ____________

2. 15 horses are in the barn.
   Some of them run away.
   8 horses are left in the barn.
   How many horses ran away? ____________

Name ____

1. 12 ducks are in the water.
   Some of them get out.
   6 ducks are left in the water.
   How many ducks got out? ______________

2. A man has 14 chickens.
   Some of them fly away.
   The man has 10 chickens left.
   How many chickens flew away? ______________

Name ______________________________

1. 19 children are in school.
   Some of them go home.
   Now there are 12 children at school.
   How many children went home? ____________

2. There are 18 birds in the tree.
   Some birds fly away.
   Now there are 9 birds in the tree.
   How many birds flew away? ________

Name ______________________________

4 children are playing.
Then more children come to play.
Now 8 children are playing.
How many children came to play? ____________

Name ______________________________

6 robins sit in a tree.

Then more robins fly to the tree.

Now 9 robins are in the tree.

How many robins flew to the tree? ____________

Name ______________________________

6 cows are in the barn.

Some horses come in.

Now there are 10 animals in the barn.

How many horses came into the barn? ____________

Name ______________________________

5 chickens are eating.
Then some more chickens come to eat.
Now there are 7 chickens eating.
How many chickens came to eat? ______________

Name ______________________________

1. A boy has 10 flowers.
   His mother gives him more flowers.
   Now the boy has 18 flowers.
   How many flowers did his mother give him? ______

2. 11 boys are running.
   Some girls come to run.
   Now there are 14 children running.
   How many girls came to run? ______________

Name ______________________________

1. 6 red apples are in a bag.
   Then a boy puts some green apples in the bag.
   Now there are 16 apples in the bag.
   How many green apples are in the bag? ________

2. 10 birds are in the garden.
   Some rabbits come to the garden.
   Now there are 12 animals in the garden.
   How many rabbits came to the garden? ________

Name ______________________________

1. 15 ducks are in the water.
   Then some more ducks fly to the water.
   Now 19 ducks are in the water.
   How many ducks flew in? ____________

2. A girl plays with 3 dolls.
   Her brother comes with more dolls.
   Now the children are playing with 13 dolls.
   How many dolls did the boy have? ____________

Name ______________________________

1. 11 big dogs are on a hill.
   Then some little dogs run up the hill.
   Now there are 17 dogs on the hill.
   How many little dogs ran up the hill? ____________

2. 8 balls are in a box.
   A baby puts more balls in the box.
   Now there are 11 balls in the box.
   How many balls did the baby put in the box? ____________

Name ______________________________

Some horses are in the barn.

3 more horses run to the barn.

Now there are 7 horses in the barn.

How many horses were in the barn at first? ________

Name ____________________

Some cakes are on the table.

A boy comes with 5 more cakes.

Now there are 8 cakes on the table.

How many cakes were on the table at first? ________

Name ____________________

Some pigs are playing.

3 more pigs go to play.

Now there are 9 pigs playing.

How many pigs were playing at first? ____________

Name ______________________________

Some birds are in a tree.

3 more birds fly to the tree.

Now there are 6 birds in the tree.

How many birds were there at first? ______________

Name ____

1. A farmer has some eggs.
   Then he finds 8 more eggs.
   Now he has 15 eggs in all.
   How many eggs did he have at first? ____________

2. A school has some chairs.
   They get 7 more chairs.
   Now they have 11 chairs in all.
   How many chairs did they have at first? __________

Name ________________________________

1. Some girls are jumping.
   4 boys come to jump.
   Now 18 children are jumping.
   How many girls were jumping? ____________

2. Some robins are in the garden.
   5 rabbits go to see them.
   Now 12 animals are in the garden.
   How many robins were in the garden? ____________

Name ______________________________

1. A bird ate some seeds.
   Then the bird ate 12 more seeds.
   The bird ate 17 seeds in all.
   How many seeds did the bird eat at first? ______

2. Some sheep are in a barn.
   Then 6 more sheep go into the barn.
   Now there are 14 sheep in the barn.
   How many sheep were in the barn at first? ______

Name ____________________

1. Some ducks are walking.
   Then 12 more ducks go to walk.
   Now there are 19 ducks walking.
   How many ducks were walking at first? ____________

2. Some rings are on a table.
   A man puts 8 more rings on the table.
   Now there are 13 rings on the table.
   How many rings were
   on the table at first? ____________

Name ______________________________

A girl has 6 toy cars.
Her brother has 2 toy cars.
The girl has how many more
toy cars than the boy? ____________

Name ______________________________

A horse eats 8 flowers.
A cow eats 3 flowers.
The horse eats how many
more flowers than the cow? ____________

Name ______________________________

There are 7 red apples.
There are 4 yellow apples.
There are how many fewer
yellow apples than red apples? ______________

Name ______________________________

There are 9 boys.

There are 7 girls.

How many fewer girls than boys are there? ________

Name ______________________________

1. A farmer finds 14 brown eggs.
   She finds 7 white eggs.
   She finds how many more
   brown eggs than white eggs? ____________

2. There are 13 dogs.
   There are 8 robins.
   How many more dogs than robins are there? ______

Name ______________________________

1. 18 trees are on a hill.
   6 bears are on the hill.
   There are how many
   more trees than bears? ____________

2. A man has 12 chickens.
   A girl has 5 chickens.
   The man has how many
   more chickens than the girl? ____________

Name ____________________

1. There are 16 red balls in a box.
   There are 5 blue balls in the box.
   There are how many fewer
   blue balls than red balls? ____________

2. There are 10 red fish.
   There are 4 green fish.
   There are how many fewer
   green fish than red fish? ____________

Name ______________________________

1. 17 sheep are in the barn.
   3 sheep are in the garden.
   How many fewer sheep are in the garden than in the barn? ____________

2. 19 robins hop.
   11 robins fly.
   How many fewer robins fly than hop? ____________

Name ______________________________

A boy has 5 balls.

He has 3 more than his mother has.

How many balls does his mother have? ____________

Name ____________________

There are 10 apples in a tree.
There are 7 more apples than robins.
How many robins are in the tree? ____________

Name ______________________________

There are 9 cows on a farm.
There are 4 fewer sheep than cows.
How many sheep are on the farm? ______________

Name ______________________________

A girl has 7 dolls.

Her brother has 6 fewer dolls.

How many dolls does her brother have? __________

Name ____________________

1. There are 20 black bears.

   There are 8 more black bears than brown bears.

   How many brown bears are there? ____________

2. There are 16 yellow fish.

   There are 5 more yellow fish than blue fish.

   How many blue fish are there? ____________

Name ______________________________

1. There are 11 little cakes.
   There are 6 more little cakes than big cakes.
   How many big cakes are there? ____________

2. A girl has 13 toys.
   She has 8 more toys than her baby brother.
   How many toys does her baby brother have? ____

Name ______________________________

1. A girl has 15 rings.
   Her father has 2 fewer rings.
   How many rings does her father have? ________

2. A boy has 12 toy cars.
   His brother has 3 fewer toy cars.
   How many toy cars does his brother have? ________

Name ________________________________

1. 19 squirrels are in a tree.
   There are 5 fewer squirrels under the tree.
   How many squirrels are under the tree? __________

2. 14 rabbits hop.
   8 fewer rabbits sleep.
   How many rabbits sleep? ______________

Word List

a
all
and
animals
apples
are
at
ate
away
baby
bag
balls
barn
bear(s)
big
bird(s)
black
blue
boat(s)
box
boy(s)
brother
brown
cakes
came
cars
cats
chair(s)
chicken(s)
children
come(s)
cow(s)
did
do
does
dog(s)
dolls
ducks
eat(s)(ing)
eggs
farm
farmer
father
fewer
finds
first
fish
flew
floor
flowers
fly
for
garden
get(s)
girl(s)
give(s)
go
got
grass
green
ground
had
has

have
he
her
hill
him
his
home
hop
horse(s)
house
how
in
into
is
jump(ing)
left
little
make(s)
man
many
more
mother
now
of

on
out
pets
pigs
play(s)(ing)
put(s)
rabbits
rain
ran
red
rest
rings
robins
run(ning)
school
see(s)
seeds
she
sheep
sit
sleep(ing)
snow
some
squirrels

stop(ped)
street
table(s)
take(s)
than
the
them
then
there
they
to
toy(s)
tree(s)
under
up
walk(ing)
water
went
were
when
white
with
woods
yellow

Correlation to Math Standards

Grade 1
Operations and Algebraic Thinking
Represent and solve problems involving addition and subtraction.
Use addition and subtraction within 20 to solve word problems involving situations of adding to, taking from, putting together, taking apart, and comparing, with unknowns in all positions, e.g., by using objects, drawings, and equations with a symbol for the unknown number to represent the problem.
Solve word problems that call for addition of three whole numbers whose sum is less than or equal to 20, e.g., by using objects, drawings, and equations with a symbol for the unknown number to represent the problem.
Understand and apply properties of operations and the relationship between addition and subtraction.
Apply properties of operations as strategies to add and subtract. Examples: *If 8 + 3 = 11 is known, then 3 + 8 = 11 is also known. (Commutative property of addition.) To add 2 + 6 + 4, the second two numbers can be added to make a ten, so 2 + 6 + 4 = 2 + 10 = 12. (Associative property of addition.)*
Understand subtraction as an unknown-addend problem. *For example, subtract 10 – 8 by finding the number that makes 10 when added to 8.*
Add and subtract within 20.
Relate counting to addition and subtraction (e.g., by counting on 2 to add 2).
Add and subtract within 20, demonstrating fluency for addition and subtraction within 10. Use strategies such as counting on; making ten (e.g., 8 + 6 = 8 + 2 + 4 = 10 + 4 = 14); decomposing a number leading to a ten (e.g., 13 – 4 = 13 – 3 – 1 = 10 – 1 = 9); using the relationship between addition and subtraction (e.g., knowing that 8 + 4 = 12, one knows 12 – 8 = 4); and creating equivalent but easier or known sums (e.g., adding 6 + 7 by creating the known equivalent 6 + 6 + 1 = 12 + 1 = 13).
Standards for Mathematical Practice
Make sense of problems and persevere in solving them.
Reason abstractly and quantitatively.
Model with mathematics.
Use appropriate tools strategically.
Attend to precision.

About the Authors

Rob Madell earned a PhD in Mathematics at the University of Wisconsin. After a brief career as a research mathematician, he became interested in elementary mathematics education and taught K–8 for 10 years at the Village Community School in New York City. He went on to work at Children's Television Workshop (Sesame Street) where he was Vice President for Interactive Technology for 15 years. He is now teaching again at Compass Charter School in Brooklyn, New York.

Laura Zoe Dombrowski earned a Master's in Educational Leadership from Bank Street College of Education. After teaching for a decade, she now works as an instructional coach, supporting teachers in their professional development.